POLLY SWEETNAM

Photo Finish

idea
Library Learning Information

To renew this item call:
0115 929 3388
or visit
www.ideastore.co.uk

TOWER HAMLETS

Created and managed by Tower Hamlets Council

MACMILLAN

Lisa works at Black and Sons.
Black and Sons is a large company.

Lisa works in the Accounts Department.
The work is very important. But it is
not very exciting.

> Your holiday is next week, Lisa.
> Are you excited?

> Oh, yes! I'm going to go
> with Alice. We're going
> to go to Greece. It will be
> fun. Perhaps something
> exciting will happen.

Alice is Lisa's friend. Alice works for Black and Sons too. She works in the Marketing Department. Alice is an artist. She designs advertisements for Black and Sons.

I want to work with Alice.
I want to work in the Marketing Department. The Marketing Department is always busy. Everybody is very friendly. They have exciting jobs.

Alice phones Lisa. They are going to get their passports today. They must go to the Post Office.

Hi, Lisa.

Hello, Alice.

Let's meet at lunch time. Then we can get our passports for our holiday.

OK. I'll meet you outside the office at 12.30.

Lisa and Alice are in the Post Office.
The assistant gives the passport
forms to the two friends.

Please fill in these forms.
Where are your passport
photos?

Here are my photos.

Oh, no! My photos
aren't in my bag! My
photos are at home!

SERVICE
Lisa, you must go to the photo booth in the old bus station. You can get your photos there.
Oh, no! I hate the old bus station. I don't want to go there.
But you must get the photos today. Listen, I can fill in the forms. Go to the bus station, Lisa. Go and get your photos. I'll wait for you here.

Nobody goes to the bus station now. There is a new bus station in the centre of town. The old bus station is empty and dark.

Lisa walks quickly. Her shoes make a loud noise on the ground.

Then she sees the photo booth. There is nobody in the photo booth. Lisa is happy. She can get her photos quickly.

Lisa goes into the photo booth. She puts her money into the machine. She closes the little curtain. She sits down. She waits.

FLASH! The camera is very quick. FLASH! FLASH! FLASH! Now Lisa can get her passport today.

EYE LEVEL

Lisa goes outside the photo booth. Her photos will come out of a slot in the machine.

Lisa hears a noise. Some photos are coming out of the slot. Are they her photos? No, it is too soon. Lisa's photos can't be ready.

But who is in the photos? There is nobody in the bus station. Nobody else is waiting for photos. Lisa is alone.

Lisa takes the photos out of the slot. There is a man in the pictures. But something is wrong. She is frightened.

The four photos show a murder!

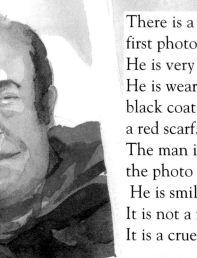

There is a man in the
first photo.
He is very large.
He is wearing a
black coat and
a red scarf.
The man is sitting in
the photo booth.
He is smiling.
It is not a nice smile.
It is a cruel smile.

The man is in
the second photo.
The man is looking
to the right.
He is afraid.

Something is
happening in the
third photo.
Somebody is holding
the man's scarf.
Somebody is
holding the man's
scarf very tightly.
The large man is
pulling at his scarf.

There is no man
in the fourth photo.
There are two hands.
The hands are
holding the
red scarf.
There is a ring
on one of the hands.
It is a strange ring.
There is a snake
on the ring.
There is a tattoo
on the other hand.
It is a tattoo of
a bird.

The hands are the murderer's hands.

Now Lisa is very frightened.

The man with the red scarf is dead. But where is his body? Where is the murderer? Is the murderer in the bus station?
The photos show the murder. The murderer knows about the photos. The murderer will come back to the photo booth. He will want the photos. I'm in danger!

Lisa and Alice are at the police station.
They are telling their story to the police.
They are showing the photos to a
detective. She is very interested.
The detective has a plan.

I know the man in
the photos. He is a
criminal. Now he
is dead. But we can
catch his murderer.

The murderer will go
back to the photo
booth. He will want
his photos. But he will
find your photos, Lisa.
He will look for you.
You can help us, Lisa.

Lisa is in the bus station. She is walking towards the photo booth. She is going to get her photos.

The police are in the bus station. They are hiding. They are watching Lisa. They are waiting for the murderer.

Lisa walks slowly.
She is very frightened.

A man is standing by the photo booth.
He is young and handsome. Is this
the murderer?

The man sees Lisa.
He smiles at her.
He has a nice smile.
He is holding some photos.
Lisa sees his hands.
She sees the snake ring.
She sees the bird tattoo!

The police catch the murderer.
The detective is pleased.
Lisa is safe.

Thank you for your help, Lisa.

Well done, Lisa! It's exciting to catch criminals.

Exciting? No! It's very frightening.

But everything is OK now. We're going on holiday. It will be fun.

Yes. Perhaps something exciting will happen!

16